Leadership Development
The Next Curve To Flatten!

by

Tom Casey and Claire Hebert-Dow

with

Deborah Hicks and Gino Piaggio Valdez

TELEMACHUS PRESS

LEADERSHIP DEVELOPMENT—THE NEXT CURVE TO FLATTEN!

Cover art and design by Telemachus Press, LLC

Published by Telemachus Press, LLC
http://www.telemachuspress.com

Visit the author's website:
http://www.discussionpartners.com

Category: BUSINESS & ECONOMICS/Human Resources & Personnel Management

ISBN: 978-1-951744-23-6 (eBook)
ISBN: 978-1-951744-24-3 (Paperback)

Version 2020.06.15

Testimonials

We currently live in strange, unprecedented times that require new thinking and proactive leadership. It is difficult to "think out of the box" when the box no longer exists. Old norms and tried-and-true past strategies may fall short amidst this new normal. Tom Casey and Claire Hebert-Dow's useful new book Leadership Development—The Next Curve To Flatten!, *offers cutting-edge help based on universal, unchanging principles, particularly suited for times like these. A valuable read to bring hope and steadiness in a unstable world.*

Stephen MR Covey
The New York Times and
#1 Wall Street Journal
Best Selling Author of
The Speed of Trust
and Co-Author of *Smart Trust*

Developing and maintaining leadership capabilities is a non-negotiable skill for those considering a change in careers or perhaps self-employment. **Leadership Development—The Next Curve To Flatten!** *Over delivers on why leadership will be ever more important going forward than it was before most people (like me) thought Corona was just a beer.*

Paul E. Casey
Author of. *Pre-Flight Checklist: Is Self Employment for You?*
Host and Producer: *Voices of Experience.Com Radio and Podcast*

In his new book **Leadership Development—The Next Curve To Flatten!**, *Tom Casey and his co-authors supply the colors and texture for the post-coronavirus leadership canvas. Leaders will need to bring their full selves to their communications with employees to inspire them to deliver the agility and collaboration required for sustained performance and prosperity. The authors show how history's lessons learned can light the way through the ambiguous, risky terrain of the new global marketplace. Above all the leader of the future must balance self-awareness with a quiet confidence forged by business experience and insights on what must change.*

Timothy Donahue
Managing Principal
Talent Directions
Co-Author of: *Talent Readiness The Future Is Now!*

The new normal for Advisory and Education organizations will be driven by experimentation as to how our services are delivered. As the Chairman and former CEO of a global firm I am mindful of the sentiments promoted by our founder Dr. Joseph Juran who at 75 perceived his insights and protocols were important to share. Juran Global remains committed to this vision. The question before our Board and Leadership team is "how"? I have worked with Tom Casey for over a decade. I believe Discussion Partners new book on Leadership Development offers useful observations in a provocative way!

Dr. Joseph Defeo
Chairman of the Board and former Chief Executive Officer, Juran Global Inc.
Author of *Juran's Quality Essentials For Leaders*

The services provided by Meals on Wheels have never been in greater need or demand. The pandemic has required our leadership to pivot quickly in ways we never envisioned, to be fully functional from a distance, to adapt our service model in short order, and to safely and creatively meet the needs of a diverse set of stakeholders, spanning our employees, our programs, our volunteers, and all-importantly, the vulnerable seniors for whom Meals on Wheels is a lifeline. We believe the lessons learned during this period will require us to revise the ways we on-board and develop our managers as a "new normalcy" evolves. I have worked with Tom Casey for over a decade and have benefitted from his counsel and the research conducted by Discussion Partners. The book **Leadership Development—A New Curve To Flatten!** *Could not arrive at a better time to help executives think about and plan for our new world!*

Ellie Hollander

President and Chief Executive Officer, Meals on Wheels America

Former Executive Vice President and Chief People Officer, AARP

The Covid-19 Pandemic has challenged many assumptions and processes among the most important of which is how companies will develop future leaders. I have known and worked with Tom Casey and **Discussion Partners** *since 2013. Their book* **Leadership Development—The Next Curve To Flatten!** *Provides timely insight as to how we as senior leaders should address what will remain if, not intensify as our primary role—Insuring our staff has the knowledge, ability, and motivation to address strategic objectives.*

Cliff Kupchan

Chairman

Eurasia Group

Alliance Management is a Hospitality Management firm that specializes in Golf and Special Events in central Conn. We recently opened up our Golf operations under strict discipline for "safe play". This would not have been possible if our leaders did not think as a selfless community vs. "domain managers". Tom Casey is on our Board of Advisors and Discussion Partner's upcoming book resonates with how Alliance will be approaching this season. The key theme for us, and we would encourage others in the hospitality sector is "protect our customers, and employees as we enjoy the activity".

Josh McKim PGA
Founder
Alliance Management LLC

Our reality has changed. We will forever be influenced by recent events requiring focused leadership in our post-pandemic world. This new world will demand different leaders who model the timeless, universal, self-evident, and self-validating governing human capital principles. Tom, Claire, Deb, and Gino address the even more important issue of how to develop leaders in light of this change. **Leadership Development—The Next Curve To Flatten!** *provides insights with humor and irony for all organizations to consider.*

Shawn D. Moon
CEO Zerorez Franchising Systems
Former Executive Vice President Franklin Covey
Best Selling Author: *Leading Loyalty-Cracking the Code To Customer Devotion*

Tom Casey has done it again! The pressures of steering global organizations through a maze of challenges falls sternly on today's leadership. The authors of **Leadership Development—The Next Curve To Flatten!** *Provides insights and expertise that will resonate with leaders looking to develop and maintain their competitive advantage. I worked with Tom Casey when both of us were at The Concours Group and was a co-author on his first book* **Talent Readiness—The Future Is Now!** *During our years of collaboration I relied on him to ask provocative questions while never losing his sense of optimism*

Eric Seubert
Client Partner &
Portfolio Market Leader
Cogniant Corporation Technology Solutions
Author of: *Breakthrough Workforce Strategy*

PB Metro, LLC (owned by Palladin Consumer Retail Partners) is comprised of 14 Pure Barre studios in New York City, Westchester County and Long Island, with 4 more locations in development. Pure Barre is the largest barre concept in North America, and these markets are the hardest hit locations of the Covid-19 virus. Our leadership team did not exist a year ago. The onset of the Pandemic brought us together quickly as we have a shared mindset of "safety first" for our clients and staff members. This principle has allowed us to be creative in working virtually with existing customers, and to plan for a successful resumption of operations. We have worked with Tom Casey since we were founded and I believe the book he and his colleagues have created addresses what is on the mind of all leaders, "how do we keep our customers and ourselves safe" as we open back up.

Kaitlin Vandura
Chairperson
PB Metro, LLC

Tom Casey and his co-authors have captured original ideas for these unusual times. This pandemic has forced a "simulated retirement" for many throughout the world. The authors address how leadership has been demonstrated and what needs to change. An incredible read, one that should open your eyes to how executives can and should accelerate their movement to life's "next stage"

Tom Wilson
Founder and Principal
The Wilson Group
Author of: *Next Stage—In Your Retirement Create the Live You Want*

Leadership Development—The Next Curve To Flatten! Provides practical insights that are a must read for leaders who are looking to excel in these challenging times. As co-author of "Becoming a Can-Do Leader" I have engaged in lively debates with many senior executives who are trying to figure out how to adapt to the "new normal". All agree that leaders need to demonstrate new definitions of competence, commitment and courage. They also agree that we are in a step-change that provides tremendous opportunities for leaders who can embrace agility and resiliency in the face of continuous uncertainty and ambiguity.

Jamie Millard
Founder Lexington Leadership Partners
Co-author-*Becoming a Can-Do Leader: A Guide for the Busy Manager*

Table of Contents

Dedications

To all of the "C's" in my life, my grandchildren, Ada Zane, Zohy Dakota, Thomas William, and Alex Upham please commit to making the world a better place, and of course the Renners!
Tom Casey, Boston MA USA

To Conan Grace, the one person who believed in me and gave me the chance and on-going support to turn my life around. His guiding principle of "Attitude Determines Altitude" kept me focused in a sales career dominated by men and vilified for its ambiguity.
Claire Hebert-Dow, Laconia NH USA

To all the mentors and leaders who believed in me when I did not, and to my sons Ivan and Jack and my husband Tim who ground me in all I do.
Deb Hicks, Boston MA USA

To my mother and father for their continuous support and affection. To my brothers for their friendship. To Camila for her love and encouragement to fulfill my dreams. And to my grandmother Mechita for sharing her life lessons with me.
Gino Piaggio Valdez, Lima Peru

Leadership Development

The Next Curve To Flatten!

Introduction

PICTURE YOURSELF AS the star of an action movie participating in a training exercise where you are sitting in a darkened room, wearing a blindfold, while anticipating an attack.

This is a fictional portrayal of how many of us are feeling as we navigate a new way of thinking of the world and our role in it.

There are no valid comparisons beyond the Influenza epidemic of 1918 to the times we are living in presently. The Covid-19 virus has united the planet in terms of anxiety, loss and confusion. The Depression of the 1930's and the Recession of 2008, while painful, are not comparable given how we are now compelled to live our lives and the continued disruption, which will exist as we move forward.

Regardless of where you live, personal circumstances or family situation, the only certainty is uncertainty.

Many of us long for the day we can sit in a coffee shop, without a mask, having a conversation. Or be able to hug our grandchildren vs. wave from 20 feet away.

General "Chesty" Puller during the Korean War uttered the quote: "We're surrounded; that simplifies things."

In the spirit of "simplifying things," **Discussion Partners** suggests as we begin re-engaging in professional roles, our number one priority should be the development of enterprise future leaders with an intensified focus on values as well as skills.

Moreover, in the context of "flattening curves," the domain of Leadership Development requires an end-to-end reset, as our pre-virus protocols will not be successful.

The focus of this book is to provide research, challenge assumptions and provoke thinking on what, given our new reality for Leadership Development, is a way forward.

This book is not a prescriptive as to steps to be taken to address Leadership Development re-invention.

Alternatively, we encourage you to adopt the improvisation of President Franklin Roosevelt in his first 100 days during the Great Depression when he instructed his Cabinet: "Do something. If it works, do more of it. If it doesn't work, do something else."

As you embark on this journey, we suggest you think innovatively, enthusiastically and with quantum amounts of good humor!

**Tom Casey &
Claire Hebert-Dow**

Chapter 1
A Pending Curve to Flatten!

TO SAY WE live in interesting times is an understatement—appalling global loss of life, disrupted lifestyles, turbulent financial markets and permission to elbow bump requiring two yardsticks!

Welcome to our new normal. However, as we navigate these uncharted waters, **DPC** suggests we not abandon forward thinking. How will you position yourself when businesses reopen; when labor requirements go through the roof and competition for the best and the brightest demands your full attention?

In respect to Covid-19 global examples of proactive disruptive leadership does exist. On April 30th the **Washington Post** addressed the approaches taken by the leaders of St. Maarten, New Zealand, Iceland, Norway, Taiwan, and Germany. Their **values driven** decisions appear presently to have mitigated the virus damage done to their societies. It was not lost to the readers of the article that all these heads of State are women.

In the context of values there are examples like **Wal-Mart** among many who are preparing for normalcy by being proactive supporting their employees now! They recognize that when the crisis ends their engagement and motivation will be essential.

There are many examples of small businesses also being proactive both in respect to compassion and strategy for one main reason: employee retention and motivation will be post pandemic critical to their business.

As of this writing, no company has clarity regarding what, if any, support governments will provide in respect to economic contributions nor guarantees for employee safety.

A sobering consideration, recently the domestic US unemployment rate was tagged at less than 4%. The crisis has a prediction for this number to be at 12% at the end of 2020. However given the 30 Million filing for unemployment, as of April, this may be optimistic.

Discussion Partners' prediction is how companies manifest support now, will predicate how employees evaluate their employers when their enterprises are once again fully operational.

McKinsey Insights recently had a quote **DPC** believes is appropriate at this time as reinforcement of values as well as strategic sense:

> *"What leaders need during a crisis is not a predefined response plan but behaviors and mindsets that will prevent them from overreacting to yesterday's developments and help them to look ahead."*

In this construct we would suggest that absent a template for the right thing to do to be supportive, defer to a modality of doing whatever you can, with the foreknowledge that employee observe and appreciate!

Overall Labor Suggestions

As you contemplate ramping back up, we suggest you consider the following scenario:

When the Covid-19 US unemployment rate goes down, how will you fill the labor needs to pursue opportunities?

Put yourself in the position of a restaurant owner who can re-open: "Re-open with whom?" should be a question they pose hypothetically now! As importantly, "Will they want to return?", and "Will they be committed to stay"?

Leadership Suggestions

Prior to the crisis, in our Leadership Effectiveness work, **Discussion Partner Collaborative** concluded that any attempt to avoid the need to: a) build a bench within the enterprise b) manifest reluctance to self-assess incumbent deficiencies, and c) embed values concomitant to skills focus will be self-defeating.

As you re-set your Leadership Development protocols post-virus we suggest you embed the following questions as you envision your "ramp up":

I.   What skills sets will we need beyond domain proficiency to have a sustainable growth-oriented enterprise?

II. How does our current population of leaders and future leaders compare to these desired attributes?

III. How can we develop and/or hire sufficient numbers of people to address deficiencies in the above?

IV. What is the true nature of our Leadership bench in respect to Readiness?

V.   How can we be truly disruptive by aligning desired values with skills in our development efforts?

VI.   What is our contingency plan to be deployed, if necessary?

Post Covid-19 Differentiated Mindset Proficiencies

1   **Anticipation**—being able to identify trends in real time in advance of competitors that, if pursued, enhance the potential for enterprise success—*for example, an organized process for R&D investment vs. gravitation towards the loudest advocate for their idea.*

2   **Agility**—the ability to pursue multiple tracks in tandem proficiently, embedding flexibility, ongoing incorporation of lessons learned and deployment of a null hypothesis contingency if corrections are required—*for example, when to exit a business line vs. postponing the decision to avoid acknowledging failure*

3   **Alignment**—consolidation of initiatives purposely built for customers that promote their interests in a sustainable measurable manner vs. a "one-off" success decision that ultimately is short-lived, or possibly even worse, results in disenfranchisement of enterprise success—*for example, a product that may enjoy success as a "fad" but whose success horizon is truncated.*

Although it is difficult to envision at the moment, there will be an end to the Covid-19 crisis. **DPC** perceives it is a constructive use of time to begin planning for the end of the crisis while being mindful that the only rule for Leadership Development is the ones you create.

Chapter 2
Improvisation in Chaotic Times

IN FEBRUARY 2020 the world entered a period of turbulence unforeseen as we welcomed in the New Year! The global virus, a careening stock market, a likely recession and a domestic US political situation that promoted intense debate (ok, this one a carryover from 2019) were more than enough to jolt even the hardiest among us.

As we look back, as chaotic as 2020 portended to be, we will reflect on those imminent challenges as the "good old days".

There is a consulting adage when an US advisor ventures into a new country: "Remember the only rule is there are *no* rules." This insight should now be in the forefront of those tasked with navigating the new normal of Leadership Development.

In January **DPC** published a Blog **Executive Readiness—2020** based upon our research and client experience.

Executive Readiness Findings: January 2020 Status
In our ongoing work with executives on their transition plans, we found the "readiness" of their Successors to be of utmost concern.

We always pose the initial question: "Are your Successors up for the challenge?" Responses such as: "No"; "Not yet"; "Not sure"; "Hard to tell" represented the norm as we entered 2020.

DPC Advisors were somewhat cynical about the "not as strong as me sentiment". However as we dug deeper we found their concerns similar in scope.

Since the creation of our Transition Advisory service in 2013, we have now worked with over 500 executives in a variety of industries and published two books on this topic, the most recent **being Executive Transitions 2—** Leveraging Experience For Future Success!
Our findings continue to validate the perspectives of transitioning executives: Successor "readiness" is suboptimal.

Shortfalls are noted in the following areas:

Global Awareness:
Given that most of the new wave of leadership candidates began their careers during the recession of the late nineties, their ability to secure an expatriate assignment or participate in extensive international travel was significantly curtailed. Moreover, the cost-constraint mentality that existed unintentionally discouraged pan-organizational initiatives in favor of more "home grown" strategic intents. Thus, the ability to learn more about global challenges was compromised.

As we entered 2020, the above restraint continued, now even more problematic given the global world in which we live driven by geo-political, economic, technology **and now health care** dynamics.

Discussion Partners' perspective is that this lack of awareness, appreciation and sensitivity to the vagaries of the situation external to our host countries will be limiting and likely self-defeating in respect to leadership development as we exit the Covid-19 crisis.

Collaboration:

Since the late nineties, collaboration has devolved to a state of electronic touch points. Days when mission-focused teams were created and participants entered a room prepared to persuade others to their point of view are waning. The use of electronic communication is now the norm. A compelling example, of course, is Zooming as a principal interaction vehicle. This type of interface can be extrapolated easily to implications for collaborative efforts.

Entering 2020, the definition of collaboration was being subsumed by a new normal of qualified awareness and subjectivity to influence. Unfortunately post pandemic, the provenance of the information deluge and nuanced communication herald a position of bias that will further complicate the ability of executives to collaborate between and among others who do not embrace their worldview.

Written Communication:

As a Baby Boomer, I still remember the Palmer method, the Nuns' obsession with good grammar and living in fear my mother, a Masters-prepared English teacher, would review my homework. Having survived the above, I now look askance at the quality of writing offered today.

We have become executives who believe that well-presented PowerPoint decks are the bastion of good communication and the more graphics, the more forceful the argument.

The art of creating a persuasive paragraph to be incorporated into a White Paper or education treatise has suffered according to our clients. As the written sentence is how most try to understand and appreciate what is being communicated.

Post pandemic **DPC** believes there will be a communication pivot to what executives "think and believe" as they incorporate points of view and new tactics into their messaging.

It is not that PowerPoint will become obsolete. However it is anticipated that well crafted decision points, delivered forcefully in writing and/or using well-scripted video will become the norm.

Intellectual Curiosity:
One of the major concerns manifested during **DPC's** Transition Advisory work is the shared insight that beyond "headlines on the phone" and domain specific journals the next wave of executives "just don't read".

As the average age of **DPC** Advisors is 66 we have learned during our careers that C-Suite executives want to understand "how to deal with adversity" and their favored self-directed learning is via reading of Biographies and History.

During our Advisory work it is unlikely we have encountered a C-Suite executive whom hasn't read Doris Kearns Goodwin's **Team of Rivals**. Presently many executives are taking profit during the Stay In Home period to read her book **Leadership In Turbulent Times**, Meacham's book **Spirit of America**, the Beschloss book **Presidents At War** and Larson's book on Churchill, **The Splendid And The Vile**.

DPC had predicted that in 2020, before the pandemic, executives would not only continue to consume information via historical books on leadership they would also become more forthcoming in presenting their points of views via op-eds, blogs, articles and books.

We trust in our prediction and are enthusiastic for the opportunity to read these treatises particularly as they embed lessons learned during the Covid-19 crisis.

Post Covid-19 Leadership Development

The above concerns do not detract from the comprehensive work being done on Succession Planning efforts. Moreover, our clients would also stipulate that the above has to be put into the context of the "world and work," which will dramatically change post pandemic.

Our overarching conclusion as we enter a new post-pandemic world is the more holistic the development of future leaders, reinforcing values with skills via creative learning vehicles the more likely the mutually beneficial success for them and their companies.

While we are not walking back concerns about readiness in the context of "normal times," we do want to note a consideration that our clients are communicating as we contemplate having to dress more formally than sweat pants. There is an overt worry that transition of executives in the near term increases enterprise risk given what is anticipated to be a dynamic "opening" post pandemic.

There are two solution sets **DPC** is recommending with the expectation of a dynamic environment continuing at least through November 2020 during which time we hope new approaches for Leadership Development are created.

1   **2021 or Bust**—In a straightforward and transparent manner request key executives defer their departure until next year. This request has a dual concern as first, the executive is likely to have already made plans and secondly, their Successors may feel irritation. However, we would stipulate that selective utilization of this interdiction is a win-win via enterprise adaptation to circumstances, preservation of the legacy reputation of the departing executive and a benefit to the Successor in respect to a calmer onboarding.

2   **Hotel California**—There is a line in an Eagles song: "You can check out but never leave," which we feel has application to today's realities. The protocols we suggest be considered encompass two options:

    a.   Creation of a retainer relationship with key executives to insure access to knowledge and guidance for a reasonable period of time;

    b.   Creation of an "Emeritus Advisory" via an enterprise sponsored LLC, whereby transitioned executives are organized as a collaborative to provide insights as individuals and/or groups to their Successors.

DPC is of the point of view that the above are sensible approaches in an environment where it is advisable to "plan for the worst while hoping for the best" concomitant to creative experimentation for Leadership Development programs.

Chapter 3
Nostalgia or Selective Memory

THE COVID-19 SITUATION has no precedent. The devastating impact of a virus yet to be quashed; the dearth of good news from the financial markets; and the uncertainty as to how our lives will unfold with travel, human interaction and employment have yet to be determined.

I like others sometimes find it easier to stay positive when musing about my journey in life to date while pondering the future.

In pursuit of perspective that maybe the way back wasn't perfect, I would share a personal reflection.

> About a year ago, my son found himself in the hospital for an extended period. He is an active adult with two young boys and was "bored to tears."

> I visited him one Saturday and listened to him complain that there was nothing to watch on TV. Sympathetic parent that I am, and also having been laid up for an extended period in my twenties barked: "Stop your whining. At least you have cable!"

For fellow Boomers, I can imagine you are also harkening back to when your parents told you: "I had to walk five miles to school in a blizzard."

Growing up in the sixties was not always easy, but it was memorable. Looking back, we can now compare how some of our rights of passage, while not necessarily nostalgic, are striking in their difference.

An immediate difference is the use of sunscreen. Coppertone was a luxury for many. Most of us burned, peeled, burned and peeled again until Labor Day.

Seat belts were likely available but usually ignored. I have the vantage point of being the oldest of seven. Once at a party I spoke to the youngest of nine. We reminisced that on short drives in convertibles, she was positioned **above** the back seat while her older brothers held her legs. Today this would be reckless endangerment—back then, a lot of kids: one car!

Transistor radios were the form of non-visual news and entertainment, the functionality of which required a battery. The battery was as essential in its day as an outlet for an iPhone is today.

Batteries became even more of a necessity during a power outage.

I recall as the oldest being ordered to go in pursuit of a battery in the early stages of a hurricane. When my mother assertively pointed out the wisdom of this move, my father's rejoinder piped in: "You have to think long term. If he blows away, it's one less college tuition." My mother's response to me as I headed out the door: "Good luck, honey."

Now you can see the origin of my parental compassion gene!

Halloween was always an annual highlight. We sometimes went to the best candy provider three times without a costume change. I don't recall my parents having to be human x-ray machines to make sure we'd be safe gorging on our bounty.

Jimmy Kimmel would have never posted Halloween "I ate your candy" segments from our family, as 'our' candy hoard rarely survived to see the light of day.

We didn't consider candy as "junk food," more like an annual entitlement.

I have no appreciation for how many TV options we have now. When I was growing up, we only had three; and they all ended with C. For the longest time, if you had a color TV, you could only watch two shows: Bonanza and Disney.

The national news was only 30 minutes a night, probably the one aspect of growing up I miss the most!

Well in truth, I probably miss the one-speed bike. Today's transport is far too confusing!

The pace of innovation is increasing, and memories are getting shorter. I vividly recall my ten-year-old grandson spying a flip phone asking: "What's that?" I shudder to think of him being exposed to a rotary dial!

I don't recall when growing up feeling I had it easy, just the opposite.

I do reflect now as a parent and grandparent that it certainly was different, not better nor worse, just memorable.

Independent of perspective, growing up I never had to Stay in Home for weeks on end or as in the case of my granddaughter missing my Prom or Graduation while wondering when college will start.

When our children and grandchildren reflect on the Covid-19 crisis, I wonder how it will be remembered, likely with the adage "it really sucked I couldn't even", or "they made me watch Dora The Explorer 15 thousand times".

Chapter 4
Remote Working: Past Insights Influence Current Realities

THE GOOD NEWS for many of us is isolation may be coming to an end over the next several weeks. And no, we're not dreaming; but it is still independent of the dramatic changes in social interaction and economic focus we will encounter once we regain mobility.

Lessons learned from our working remotely should not be disregarded in light of our enthusiasm and relief that circumstances have changed—for the better provided we modify our behavior.

Many of us worked from home for the first time with little time to get acclimated to this new normal. This required efforts to resist the temptation to engage in our Hugh Hefner side, working in pajamas or maybe in sweat suit attire with the expectation that "maybe" we'll exercise—later.

The biggest challenge was, and for many remains, bringing discipline to day-to-day activities irrespective of imagining a commute to work being replaced by a walk to the kitchen.

In thinking through this unanticipated state of affairs, **DPC** thought it would be helpful to look at the pre-virus research on the most frequently mentioned downsides of working remotely for insights that could be embedded into an approach.

Dr. Lynda Gratton of the London Business School in her **Future of Work** research published in 2019, found the following most frequently mentioned downsides to working remotely:

1   **Unplugging After Work—22%**
2   **Loneliness—19%**
3   **Collaboration and Communication—17%**

The **MIT Sloan Management Review** on April 8 published an article entitled: "**Managing Stress and Emotions While Working Remotely**" **b**y Liz Fosslien and Mollie West Duffy.

This exceptional article identified eight consequences of working remotely. The top three suggestions were as follows:

1   **Emotionally Proofread Your Messages**—Need to recognize that circumstances may lead to unfortunate language construct. One **DPC** Partner indicated recent communication was along the lines of what he would convey to an ex-wife during a difficult day.

2   **Schedule Time for Serendipitous Collaboration**— Mindful of Doctor Gratton's research, another **DPC** Partner schedules a Zoom innovation wine hour while conceding productivity suffers "somewhat."

3   **Check in With Each Other**—It cannot be stressed enough that in many ways the need for interaction is

what we and our colleagues and relationships need the most.

Discussion Partners has relationships in many countries where the stay-at-home practices are strongly supported. For example, **Spain** where walking a dog is one of the few reasons where one can be outside. One of our Partners has a dog that is very popular with his neighbors; he recently noted the pooch is now "exhausted and asking for legal representation."

Societies such as **New Zealand** and **Peru** went into total lockdown early with at the moment positive results.

Below is a vignette from Gino Piaggio on coping in a society with a total lockdown, reinforcing what **DPC** has seen in most circumstances, the value of discipline and companionship.

Peru is under a strict quarantine, so you can only go shopping for groceries to the nearest supermarket. The curfew runs from Monday to Saturday, from 4 p.m. to 4 a.m., and on Sundays nobody can go out. The only people authorized to go to the office are those that work in the financial, journalistic and food sectors. I, as a lawyer, have to work from home.

At first, working from home wasn't easy. I don't have a scanner, a printer and a photocopier, as I do at the office. Although these tools are not essential, they make my job easier. However, over time, I got used to it.

The confinement has not affected me as much as I thought, and I think it's because I never considered the quarantine a vacation. I get up at 8 a.m., as always, and after breakfast, I get rid of my pajamas and start working. At 2 p.m., after having lunch, I read for an hour and then do some exercise. Once I'm done exercising, I take a shower and continue working. At the end of the day, I have dinner, watch a movie and read until I get tired. Usually, I go to sleep at midnight.

I'm lucky because I'm not alone in this quarantine: My mother and grandmother are by my side. I talk to them whenever I can, especially during breakfast and lunch, and on weekends we play cards, cook something special and have a nice time together.

During this period of forced at-home via contact with clients and within the **DPC** community, the following principles have evolved:

- **Think Selfishly**—Work means work without distraction to promote value. While it is counterintuitive to be at home with family whom you have to ignore, it is a necessity. Hopefully, disciplined structure for day-to-day time can address the ambiguity of "going to my kitchen office and can't be disturbed."

- **Learning Laboratory**—In the process of surviving and trying to be productive, one of our derivative insights relates to its being a good time to read. Recent books on Lincoln, Churchill and FDR have risen in emotional value. We offer this suggestion in an effort to help you avoid the consequence of streaming as a way of life.

- **The Ten-Year Look-Back**—Most of us think of our careers on a three-to-five-year sequence. At present, this mindset smacks headfirst into the reality of "*Life Is Too Short.*" **DPC** urges consideration of a different mental model to avoid angst and overreactions on career decisions. Our suggestion is to envision a longer-term future and begin making preliminary plans.

- **Think Ironically**—The best antidote to preoccupation
  with difficult circumstances is to look for the humor in
  any situation. In this spirit, the following is offered from
  a **DPC** Partners call on the impact of working remotely:
    - ✓ I no longer need to read the subtitles when
      streaming Norwegian crime dramas on Netflix;
    - ✓ I am writing a pilot for Survivor Costco;
    - ✓ I enjoy meaningful conversations with my
      household appliances;
    - ✓ I am working on a project plan for the
      distribution of paper products;
    - ✓ I hear my husband mutter daily: "My mother
      was right about her."

Bill Gates, whose foundation is funding many vaccine research
initiatives, indicated there would be no automatic reset from working
remote to automatic resumption of normal work habits.

DPC takes the view that our shared experience has some value if we
reflect on how we approached our circumstances and willingness to
embed the positive aspects into our moving-forward work habits.

Chapter 5
Post Pandemic Role of Executive Coach

AS WE ENTERED 2020, the Executive Coaching sector was in transition. As we emerge from the Stay At Home mandate, the proliferation of those who portray their service offering as "coach" along with the number of "certification" programs will be assaultive as displaced executives and those who emerge looking for fundamental career change decide to be a "Coach".

Discussion Partners began tracking the evolution of Executive Coaching at the onset of the 2008 global recession. Its impetus was based on the fact many seasoned displaced executives had positioned themselves as "coaches" given their then lack of employment opportunities. **DPC** posted its first blog on the topic in 2009. The impetus for the first blog was the feedback we had been receiving from C-Suite clients on their level of dis-satisfaction with the service offering and value it added to their enterprise.

Their overarching feedback was: "It depends more on the coach than the assignment." We perceive this sentiment will continue as a success prism in the foreseeable future post pandemic.

The focus of this chapter is to convey the findings that have evolved over ten years of monitoring this dimension of Leadership Development.

To reinforce the introspection for those contemplating becoming a coach post pandemic, we thought it helpful to share the sentiments of a celebrated executive. Having just retired while considering this career path she asked: "How do I differentiate myself as an Executive Coach?"

Deb Hicks recently retired from her executive leadership position as the most senior Human Resources officer from Dana Farber Cancer Institute at the end of a distinguished career in the health care sector to start her next chapter. She writes:

> *The primary challenge of a senior executive becoming an Executive Coach after a career "inside" rests on differentiating oneself from the current cadre of coaches.*
>
> *In order to organize my thinking on this next chapter, I focused on my career purpose and passion for being a trusted advisor while balancing my time with other interests.*
>
> *It was the component of my role as a trusted advisor where I found the greatest satisfaction and joy in my work.*
>
> *In order to differentiate myself, I am focusing on deeper education, concentrating on learning how others advance leadership skills to improve their lives, and the careers and lives of those they impact.*

I trust my experience and associated networks and relationships, supported by this educational framework, will justify an organization's decision to choose me as their Coaching Advisor.

Deciding to pursue this avenue was a choice to embark on a road not yet traveled for myself, one of creativity and courage. It was also time to ask the question: "If not now, when?"

I am challenged and excited to pursue new learning and growth for myself while in support of my clients and their organizations.

Post Pandemic the domain of Executive Coaching will grow rapidly for three incongruent reasons. Foremost, it has been well researched and documented the use of *external* coaches is **the** most impactful leadership development vehicle. Secondly, with the transition of so many "Boomer" executives, there will continue to be an increase of those carrying the business card of Executive Coach. Finally due to the Covid-19 Pandemic it is highly likely there will be more executives wanting to be "coaches" due to displacement or personal choice to "do something different as life is too short".

With respect, but an abundance of caution, post pandemic as was he case during the 2008 recession, well-intentioned, but unprepared, advisors will begin referring to themselves as "coaches". Absent a recognized degree or certification the establishment of baseline criteria is advisable.

This is of particular importance as Executive Coaching will be such an important strategy as we re-invent Leadership Development migrating towards a values and skills interdiction.

During our over ten years of research on the topic, we have focused on C-Suite feedback: "To be impactful, what are the top five critical skills needed by an effective executive coach?"

Top 5 Responses

- **Strong Business Fundamentals**—Many coaches focus on strategy and operations, whereas others focus on leadership effectiveness. The response had more to do with a third area in that even when advising on the quality of a leadership bench, or correcting some less than attractive behaviors, there is a need for the coach to know enough about the market forces in which the client company competes to be credible to those being supported and the senior deciders.

    As we exit the Pandemic, it is now more important than ever knowledge of geopolitical and macro-economics is a "must!"

- **Sensei Tendencies**—The ability of the coach to weave in "war stories" or "lessons learned" from their experience. At **Discussion Partners** we refer to this as *Illustration Advisory*, an intervention whereby we can share an example. There is, of course, the need to resist the temptation to pontificate on "when I was a young manager."

    CEOs have been, and post pandemic will be, asking for an advanced script on how the coach intends to help manage their incumbent move beyond personal experience, migrating more toward an education model with lessons learned, historical examples and other client—experience foundations.

- **Willingness to Confront**—The desire to avoid offending to preserve economic security can be taken too far in a relationship. There can be diplomatic ways to articulate: "What were you thinking?" In reality it is mandated this form interaction be deployed when necessary.

- **Intellectual Foundation**—This attribute initially surprised us at **DPC**; however it is only logical that a sponsoring client be entitled to expect their advisor to remain current. Although John Boudreau, Noel Tichy, David Ulrich, Jim Collins and Michael Porter are in a class by themselves, the reputation of the coach can be enhanced if they share insights from others as well as their own documented point of view. Of particular interest post-pandemic is an awareness of the thoughts on leadership by historians such as Doris Kearns-Goodwin, Michael Beschloss and Jon Meacham.

    CEOs also prefer coaches who have an organized fact-based point of view preferably demonstrated through thoughtful leadership via speeches, op-ed pieces, blogs and publications.

- **Willingness to Admit Failure**—Staying in a bad marriage is counterproductive if not counterintuitive. The same logic applies to a coaching relationship. If it isn't working, the coach should be the initiator of the relationship separation. Anything less is suboptimal for the client and candidly, an unfair position for an enterprise sponsor.

You will note there is a presumption of a methodology and highly attuned interactive skills! Both are considered to be threshold attributes by CEOs.

Given the likely expansion of those calling themselves an Executive Coach, the above is offered as a point of view to assist you in what **DPC** refers to as QQ (Qualification/Quality) decisions and utilization post pandemic as Leadership Development protocols are rethought, refined, and re-invented.

Chapter 6
The Pirate Paradox—Lessons Learned Via Embarrassment

CONSULTANTS LOVE ACRONYMS. It helps us organize our thinking; reinforce points to clients in stark terms; and in the realm of self indulgence sometimes makes us think we are smart!

Of course, it can have a downside!

As we re-engage with our associates post virus with its stay-at-home challenges, we should be mindful of one of the major lessons learned during this period: social interaction with associates is a vacuum, which you as the leader must fill.

In the spirit of correcting a deficiency in my leadership style, I coined the term "VAR" to promote self-awareness:

- **Visibility**—representation to the enterprise through presence, not symbolic, but rather tactical—inclusive of decision-making in real time and as importantly, "in person."

- **Access**—promotion of an image whereby peers and subordinates are encouraged to approach with requests for guidance or reality checks
- **Responsiveness**—assertiveness in closing the loop on requests, clearly avoiding having to be asked twice!

The personally embarrassing episode was when in the office on a Friday I was confronted by an employee who was "introducing himself."

The discourse went something like this ...
1 **"Hi, Tom. I'm Brian."**
2 **"Hi, Brian. How are you doing?"**
3 **"Good. It has been interesting."**
4 **"That's good to hear. How long have you been here?"**
5 **"About four months."**
6 **"So, who do you report to?"**
7 **"Actually you, Tom."**

I created the VAR tool initially for myself and have over the years used it with associates and clients as well.

This led to the Pirate Paradox: "As if you say, 'VAR' real fast as one of my Partners ventured, you sound like you're Long John Silver. All that's missing is the parrot on your shoulder."

Allusions to Treasure Island aside, for clients and myself with whom I have referenced the acronym, it is a not-so-gentle reminder that the Woody Allen comment "80% of success is showing up" has merit.

Post Covid-19 if you believe that you are not sufficiently visible with those with whom you should be, particularly after our respective stay-at-home experience, think of VAR.

Be advised that if you find yourself sharing VAR, say it slow to avoid being called "Matey."

Chapter 7
Anchor vs. Outlet

AS WE ENTERED 2020 the year already portended to be an interesting time for the following reasons:

- Europe was beginning to cope with Brexit
- Upcoming US presidential election;
- Asia dealing with tariffs and
- South America focusing on constitutional crisis in several societies

The onset of the Covid-19 overtook the above and other difficult matters due to global preoccupation with health and economic realities.

In the interest of thinking about something, maybe anything else, as we emerge from Stay At Home, for executives who just prior and now contemplating transition, **DPC** would encourage you consider the following.

DPC reinforces with executives in transition the difference between the "anchors" they have often taken for granted as opposed to the "outlets" where their interests and energies will focus in the years ahead.

The Anchor Concept

We identify an **Anchor** as those influences which have most contributed to career satisfaction. For example:

- **Family**—Pride in how their families have grown and prospered due to the success they generated during their career, such as providing access to a quality education.

- **Learning**—Recognition that personal success has been influenced by their own educational achievements whether in formal academics, intellectual pursuit, professional and life experiences.

- **Feedback**—Satisfaction derived from the positive reinforcement received from those whose careers and outlooks you influenced during your leadership tenure (be advised this is not to be confused with insincere "happy talk")

Successful executives "keep commercial score" through title, position, compensation and individual brand prestige. However, when queried as to how they keep "personal score," the above three drivers are emphasized.

The Outlets Concept

In discussion of *what's next*, beyond the obvious desire to "stay relevant," "maintain intellectual edginess" and "control over calendar," the following are most often referenced:

- **Visibility**—Involvement with initiatives where presence is not symbolic but tactically inclusive in real time decision-making.
- **Access**—Promotion of an image whereby peers and interested parties are encouraged to approach with requests needing a thoughtful and experience-based response.
- **Responsiveness**—Assertiveness on the part of others in closing the loop on requests, avoiding the need to be asked twice to heed the need for executive involvement.

The activities of Board memberships, Angel investors, NGO involvement, etc. as well as Advisory resource are likely post-career endeavors.

Post pandemic we believe many executives will transition or possibly modify their current role. We strongly suggest that this journey is a thoughtful progression vs. "change for the sake of change absent a plan".

Please be mindful that those coming behind you are observing and if not now, will eventually make decisions influenced by how you approach your own situation.

Chapter 8
Going Last Can Also Be Fun!

PRIOR TO THE outbreak of Covid-19 I had have been on the road since May promoting our most recent book, **Executive Transitions 2—Leveraging Experience For Future Success!** with speeches in the States, Europe, and South America.

Since the onset of the outbreak I never thought I would miss hotel viewing of my traveling companions **CNN** and **BBC**.

Last year I had been following the news on the 50-year commemoration of Woodstock. I remember the "Live Action News" being broadcast at the time of the event as well as the movie when it first came out.

One of my recollections from the movie, and a lesson learned transitioned to my speaking engagements is "no way do you want to go last"! I remember Jimi Hendrix insisted on going last, as the wont of most musicians, and played on a Monday morning to about 1/3 of the concert attendees and many vendors picking up the garbage.

For those of you who give speeches and presentations, you know the best "slot" is the Keynote, or on a Panel with people who don't argue with your data set or point of view.

Last is not a desired spot as you are often presenting to a smaller group whom if attending are holding the handles to their luggage ready to bolt for the airport.

I did learn a trick that has helped when circumstances dictate that last is your slot.

I was home in Boston, during a time when a National Association was holding their annual meeting. Coincidentally I was at their hotel for another meeting when a friend who was on the Association Board came up to me with the words, "Tom, our closing speaker can't get out of Chicago due to weather, can you speak". The man is a good friend, and so I agreed, reluctantly!

My intro was an apology, "I am sorry to be your back up speaker and even more sorry that Steven Tyler from Aerosmith was un-available: but if you all stay to the end I will lead you all in singing Dream On". They stayed, we sang, much to the surprise of the hotel staff the harmonies didn't suck!

I had a more recent experience where due to a delayed flight my slot was bumped to last. The audience was kind enough to stay, albeit with their carry-ons close by their side.

In my apologetic opening I suggested if they could bear to stay through the speech I would lead the group in the Queen song We Are the Champions! Surprisingly they did stay, most likely out of curiosity. I did lead the group in the song, including the clapping, foot stopping opening.

Never let it be said that a group of Industrial Psychologists can't sing in harmony or eschew playing air guitar!

Preference is just that it is one's comfort zone, circumstances oftentimes are uncontrollable, unless one adapts, our post pandemic way of life.

I have been speaking and presenting on various topics for decades, and have learned that audiences, clients, colleagues, and peers with few exceptions want to hear what you have to say, and appreciative of your effort in sharing insights.

As we leave home in pursuit of securing a table at the local Starbucks, and I hopeful that I will give another speech be mindful that we as leaders will be under scrutiny as to how we embed the lessons learned due to the crisis influence our style.

In the spirit of President Roosevelt's dictum during his first Cabinet meeting, to be proactive, as it relates to Leadership Development **DPC**, would encourage you to tune up your air guitar and get creative!

All that came before in terms of how you were viewed as a leader is now irrelevant What you do next is how you will be remembered.

Chapter 9
Time to Look in the Mirror!

AS HAS BEEN said by many the Covid-19 crisis has brought out the "best and worst" in the human race. The selfless courage of our first responders, health care professionals, and those, whose more straightforward roles put them at risk so we could emerge from the pandemic safer, should never be forgotten. For those who fought over toilet paper and other behaviors that were shameful, you will be ridiculed and soon an unpleasant memory.

In 2016 Discussion Partners published **Executive Advice to The Young—Don't Repeat My Mistakes!**

For this book I interviewed a Boston based gentleman whom previously had an extensive career in the US military as a Special Operations Officer.

The executive was then commenting on the polarizing debate within the US on immigration and fearful that it would lead to a societal overreaction.

The interview was as follows—

September 11th changed much for us in the States. We no longer felt safe, and for the most part unclear who was the enemy as in decades past it was clear and now it is a religious belief kidnapped by extremists for their own purposes.

I have to say though that in the aftermath I behaved very badly on one specific occasion for which I am still ashamed.

About a week after 9/11 I boarded a plane from Boston to Dallas. I was upgraded to First Class, as the plane was somewhat empty.

Shortly after I boarded another passenger came on who looked of Arabic descent. I gave him a look that at best could be described as rage if not overtly threatening.

Immediately after he took his seat, also in First Class I took off my belt, rolled it up into a garrote, and covered it with my jacket. Candidly I don't know what I would have done if he had moved towards the cockpit, likely something stupid.

Fortunately he did not get out of his seat. When we landed, I felt awful and guilty.

I waited for him in the terminal and apologized for the look I gave him with the words. I am sorry, that was inappropriate, and I thought I was better then that.

The man was startled that I took the time, he was Iranian and had come to the States as a student in the 80's and never went back due to the change in leadership and society culture.

He did say "I guess I have to get used to people being suspicious and focusing their anger on me—I am angry too for what has been done to us!"

When asked for his thoughts on the above he stipulated:

- *I remember most he used the word us! This man felt the same way I did about the terrorist attack.*
- *It is dangerous to blame a society, religion, or philosophy for the actions of a few who interpret by self indulgence*
- *Other than Native Americans all in the US have immigrant origins the only question is how many generations between our ancestors and us ignoring this or forgetting is self serving at best*

Presently the blame game seems to be alive and insidiously well as we navigate the Pandemic. There is much to be learned in terms of what happened, what could have been done differently, who was accountable, how can we self-correct to avoid a repetition etc.

In the context of Leadership Development regardless of where we, and the next generation leaders sit, we should be mindful that introspection, acknowledgement of judgment lapses, are just as much skills as they are values.

Chapter 10
Conclusion: Even Monkeys Fall Out of Trees!

DPC HAS BEEN fortunate for seven years to work closely with a large global consumer products company. In a conversation with one of their Tokyo-based executives, he referenced the Japanese saying, *'even monkeys fall out of trees!"*

The saying is prophetic for many reasons, among which is relevance to our shared Covid-19 experience.

When you contemplate the saying, your intuitive reaction is to think, "poor monkey," while conjecturing, "what does the monkey do now?"

There are a number of options:

1   **NFL Penalty**—This is when the monkey becomes a drama student insisting "what me?" similar to the Oscar performances one sees among penalized defensive players.

2   **Woe Is Me**—This is when the monkey looks for an audience who embraces their self-pity.

3   **Blaming the Tree**—This is when somehow the tree moved without informing the monkey.

4   **Paralyzing Indecision**—This is when the monkey ponders, "Not sure trees are for me. Maybe I should learn to swim."

A monkey being a monkey, they realize the tree is their home and the most conducive environment for their success.

However, what becomes the new post-fall reality? Do they wear a parachute, strap themselves to the tree or accept the ambiguities of existence while exercising an abundance of caution?

As we progress further into our post-virus world, accepting the ambiguity associated with the turbulence leaves two avenues for pursuit. One can play it safe, or accept risk and go for it!

As leaders who have the responsibility to focus on the development of the future generation, it compels us to metaphorically self-assess: What type of monkey do I want to be?

Post SIH we all will have war stories and insights. Claire, Deb, Gino and I would actively encourage you to reflect and embed into your development models only the legitimate and useful lessons learned. It will be difficult to smile and stay positive in the immediate future. Suck it up. Our ability to look forward is why we have the job in the first place.

There is a quote from Winston Churchill that is appropriate for our Covid-19 reality, and the challenging of Leadership Development we endorse. "Now is not the end. It is not even the beginning of the end. But perhaps it is the end of the beginning".

Other Books by Tom Casey

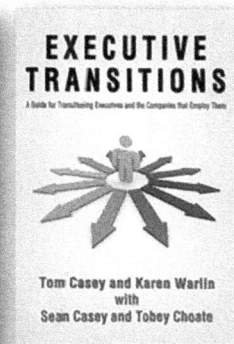

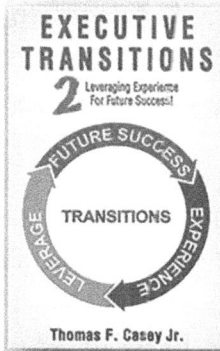

Author Biographies

Tom Casey

Tom Casey is the Managing Principal of Discussion Partner Collaborative LLC (www.discussionpartners.com) a global Executive Advisory firm. He is the author of over 400 articles and blogs and 7 previous books 4 of which have been classified as best sellers by various associations. His most recent book was **Executive Transitions 2—Leveraging Experience For Future Success**. During his 45 plus years of consulting he has been associated with Harbridge House Inc., Arthur D. Little, PricewaterhouseCoopers, and The Concours Group. Tom is a retired Special Operations officer having served in both the US Air Force and Army. He holds a Bachelors Degree from the University of Alaska, MA and MBA degrees from Rivier University. He also graduated from the Yale University Executive Management Program. Tom can be reached at:
tcasey@dpcadvisors.com

Claire L. Hebert-Dow

Ms. Hebert-Dow is a proud native and lifelong resident of the Lakes Region in New Hampshire. Having earned a BA in Psychology with Summa Cum Laude and Phi Beta Kappa honors from the University of New Hampshire, she embarked on a 25-year sales career with Mutual of Omaha achieving awards across all three of her licenses of health, life and securities.

Following retirement, she returned to academia completing a Masters in English and Creative Writing from Southern New Hampshire University and is currently in the midst of completing her memoir, sales of which will be directed to service K-9's. Her recent writing credits include work for Square Spot Studio for annual edit of Tilton School alumni magazine and human interest stories for the Laconia Daily Sun. Claire can be reached at:

clairehebert8@icloud.com

Contributors

Deborah Hicks

Before starting her own Consulting and Leadership Coaching practice, Deb had a distinguished career in HR executive leadership roles which included: SVP, Chief People and Culture Officer at Dana-Farber Cancer Institute, Associate Dean and Chief HR Officer at Harvard Medical School, and Vice President of HR at Harvard Pilgrim Health Care.

Additionally, Massachusetts' Governor Charlie Baker appointed Deb, to serve as Co-Chair of his Human Resources transition team. Deb was awarded the John D. Erdlen Award for demonstrating excellence in Human Resources through her leadership and out-standing contribution to the profession. Deb currently serves as a mentor for MIT's Venture Mentoring Service supporting innovations and entrepreneurship at MIT, and has served on a variety of Boards. Deb is a graduate of the University of Massachusetts and holds a Masters Degree from Antioch College. Deb can be reached at: deb_hicks@comcast.net

Gino Piaggio Valdez

Gino Piaggio Valdez is an attorney with the Valencia Law Office in Lima, Peru. He is a member of the Peruvian Association for Industrial Property and Copyrights. Gino obtained both his first and law degrees from the Universidad de Lima, in Lima, Peru. He has completed a short fiction stories book titled 'It's A Beautiful World' and is presently writing a fiction novel tentatively titled 'Pandemic' to be published in 2021. One of his short stories, titled 'Tucson', won the award for best short story given by the master of creative writing of the Universidad Catolica del Peru. He is also the co-author with Tom Casey of the best seller **Executive Advice to the Young—Don't Repeat My Mistakes!** Gino can be reached at: ginopiaggio@hotmail.com

www.ingramcontent.com/pod-product-compliance
Lightning Source LLC
Chambersburg PA
CBHW022017190326
41519CB00010B/1548